GRAMMAR RAY
PREPOSITIONS

a graphic guide to grammar
andrew carter

Published by Evans Brothers Limited
2A Portman Mansions
Chiltern Street
London W1U 6NR

© in this edition Evans Brothers Limited 2010
© in the text and illustrations Andrew Carter 2010

Printed in Malta by Gutenberg Press

Editor: Sophie Schrey
Designer: Mark Holt

British Library Cataloguing in Publication Data

Carter, Andrew.
Prepositions. — (Grammar Ray)
1. English language—Prepositions—Juvenile literature.
I. Title II. Series
425.7-dc22

ISBN-13: 9780237538514

contents

INTRODUCTION

Hello and welcome to Grammar Ray! You are
about to enter a world of fun and adventure, where
English grammar is brought to life. Words in the English
language can be divided into different groups called
'parts of speech'. In this title, we will join some
weird and wonderful creatures and explore
the role of prepositions.

We live in the Zoo of Prepositional
Creatures. Come inside to see us in
action – we do lots of amazing things!

The first part of this book is a comic strip.
Join the prepositional creatures inside the zoo
and witness some astonishing behaviour.
Look out for the words in yellow - they
are key to our visit.

After you've explored inside the zoo the
rest of the book looks at prepositions in more
detail, and gives some more examples. Use this
if you need a reminder of the role prepositions
play in the English language. It also requires
your puzzle solving skills, and tests what
you have learnt along the way.
So be sure to pay attention!

First let's look at some prepositions that can tell us about movement.

Over

It jumped over the gap.

Up

It flies up to the food.

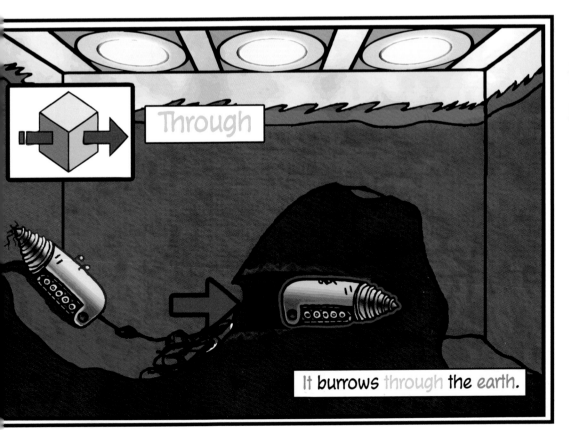

Through

It burrows through the earth.

Off

They glide off the cliff.

Next, let's look at some prepositions that tell us about location.

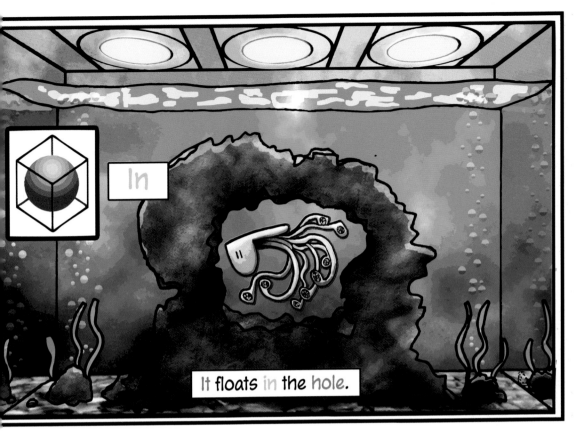

It floats in the hole.

The creatures float above the clouds.

In winter

They love to ski in winter.

During prehistory

These creatures lived during prehistory.

These creatures only come out at night.

A Guide To Prepositional Creatures Of The World

By
Peter Wreppo
and
Cynthia Zishon

Chameleug (Prepuis Simulo)

Chameleugs live in rock pools on the coasts of
Southern Japan. These prepositional creatures are
difficult to find because they are very clever at
camouflaging themselves. Once they have slithered
onto a surface, chameleugs mimic the colour and texture
almost exactly (figure 1). This means that when
predators fly over them, they are almost invisible.

Left: Chameleugs often carry
their young on their backs.
The little ones sit beside
each other.

Figure 1.

Octograb (Prepuis Penitusmolluscacaverna)

Octograbs live in the ocean and look similar to squids and octopuses. They hide themselves away from sight in a small nook or cave and wait for an unsuspecting crustacean to pass by (figure 1). Once a victim has been sighted above or below, an octograb will reach out with its long tentacles and clasp its prey before quickly eating it up (figure 2)!

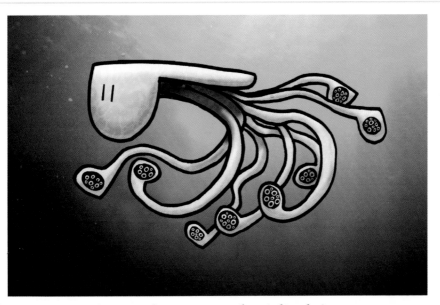

Above: a rare image of an octograb sighted in open water.

Figure 1.   Figure 2.

Speelie (Prepuis Ranunculusvertere)

Speelies can be found on the salt plains of Bolivia. They have a wheel that enables them to move rapidly around any fast moving prey, making it dizzy (figure 1). Once the speelie has trapped its target, a long frog-like tongue darts from its mouth and snatches the disorientated prey (figure 2).

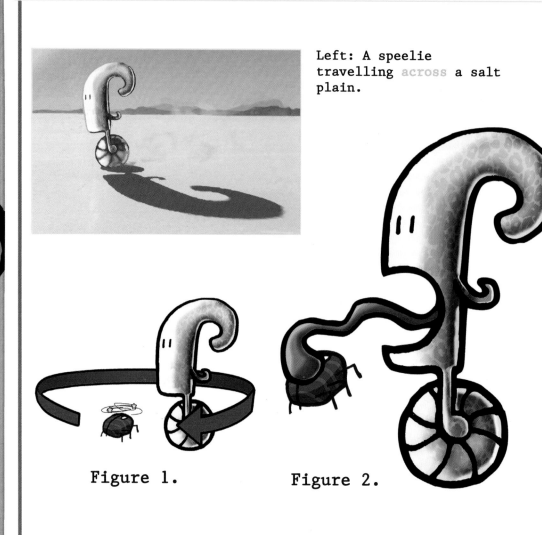

Left: A speelie travelling across a salt plain.

Figure 1.   Figure 2.

Flutterbloat (Prepuis Papiloanimosus)

Flutterbloats live in the forest. They can be found on tree branches in South America. Flutterboats breathe in air to inflate themselves like tiny balloons (figure 1). Their wings guide them through the air. They fly up very high as they search for food on the branches above (figure 2). At night flutterboats are particularly active.

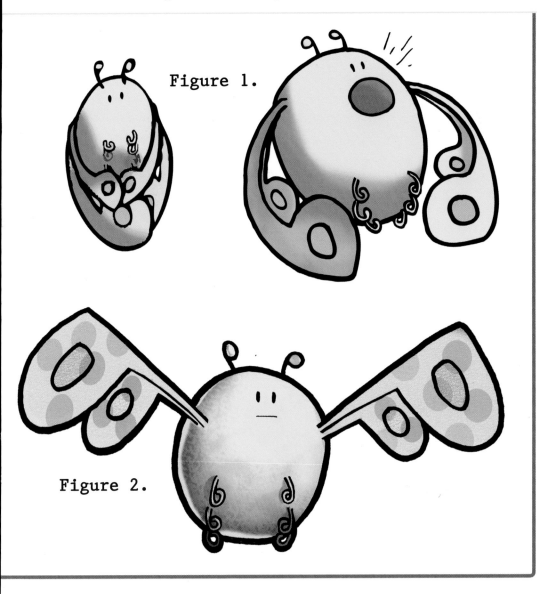

Figure 1.

Figure 2.

prepositions

Prepositions are small words that link nouns and pronouns in a phrase or sentence.

FOR EXAMPLE:

The ogre lived <u>between</u> the two mountains
  (NOUN)   (PREPOSITION)   (NOUN)

In this sentence, the preposition 'between' tells us where the ogre lived. It provides a link between the nouns 'ogre' and 'mountains'.

Prepositions are always part of a phrase or sentence. When used on their own, they do not have any specific meaning. If we saw the word 'between' on its own we would ask 'between what', or 'between where'?

Prepositions tell us about the movement and location of nouns and pronouns.

PREPOSITIONS OF MOVEMENT

up, off, over, through, around, down, in, into

FOR EXAMPLE:

The tired fish swam <u>down</u> to the seabed.

She put the milk <u>into</u> the fridge.

The car went <u>through</u> the tunnel.

The frog jumped <u>over</u> the hole.

PREPOSITIONS OF LOCATION

in, on, under, behind, beside, above, below, by, near, between

FOR EXAMPLE:

The boy hid <u>behind</u> the sofa.

The pirates sat <u>under</u> the palm trees drinking rum.

The giant lives <u>beside</u> the mountain.

The magician was <u>on</u> the stage one minute, but gone the next.

Prepositions can also be used with certain nouns to tell us about time.

PREPOSITIONS OF TIME

In spring, at once, during summer, on Halloween.

FOR EXAMPLE:

It started to snow <u>on</u> Christmas Eve.

<u>At</u> twelve o'clock the huge clock chimed.

The zoo is open <u>during</u> the day.

Sometimes prepositions can contain two or three words. These are known as complex or compound prepositions.

COMPLEX PREPOSITIONS

next to, in front of, near to

FOR EXAMPLE:

I sat <u>next to</u> my friend.

His glasses were right <u>in front of</u> him.

prepositions
test yourself

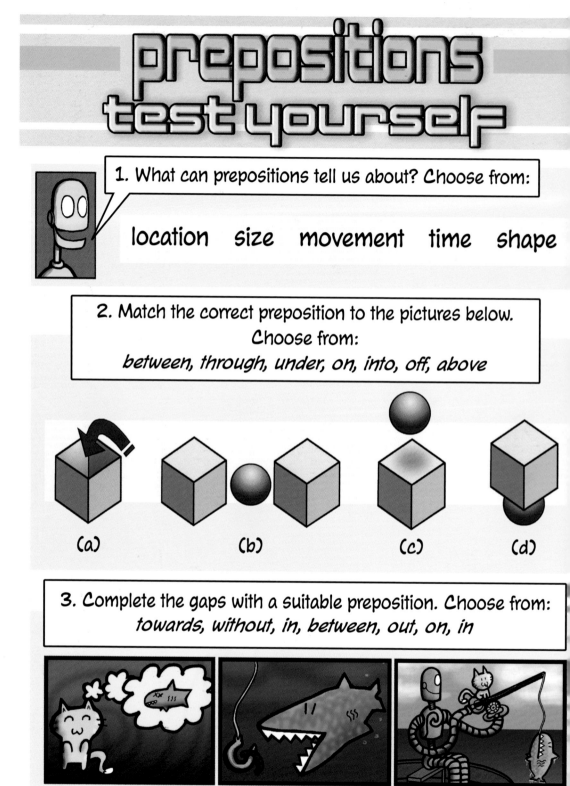

1. What can prepositions tell us about? Choose from:

location   size   movement   time   shape

2. Match the correct preposition to the pictures below.
Choose from:
between, through, under, on, into, off, above

(a)   (b)   (c)   (d)

3. Complete the gaps with a suitable preposition. Choose from:
towards, without, in, between, out, on, in

(a) The cat saw a delicious fish __ its dream.
(b) A worm was __ the hook as the fish swam _____ it.
(c) The robot reeled __ the line and lifted the fish ___ of the water.

4. Which prepositional creature is best suited to complete each obstacle course?

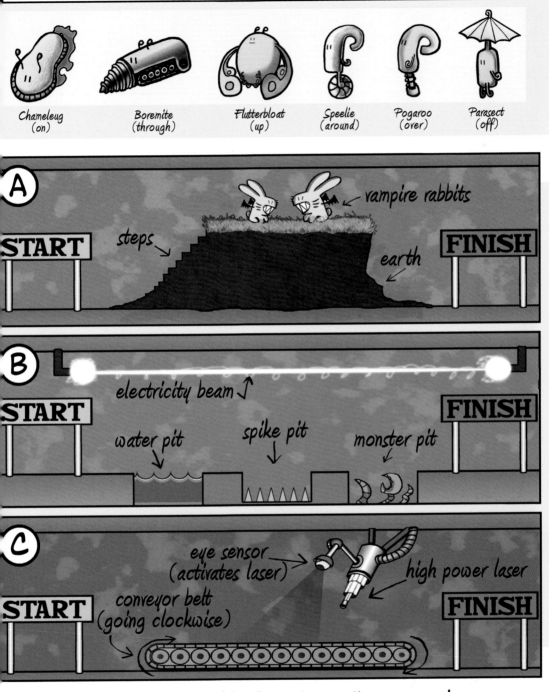

Chameleug (on)

Boremite (through)

Flutterbloat (up)

Speelie (around)

Pogaroo (over)

Parasect (off)

A
START
steps
vampire rabbits
earth
FINISH

B
electricity beam
START
water pit
spike pit
monster pit
FINISH

C
eye sensor (activates laser)
conveyor belt (going clockwise)
high power laser
START
FINISH

Turn the page upside-down to see the answers!

1. location, movement, time. 2. (a) into (b) between (c) above (d) under
3. (a) in (b) on, towards (c) in, out
4. (A) Boremite digs through the earth to safety (B) Pogaroo hops over
(C) Chameleug can become invisible on the conveyor belt and avoid the laser

23

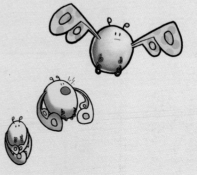